Here is the story of Captain James Cook, who was one of the greatest sailors, explorers and navigators ever to sail from the shores of England. He was one of the first of the really scientific navigators, and his work made great contributions to many fields of knowledge besides geography.

Captain Cook

written and illustrated by FRANK HUMPHRIS

Ladybird Books Loughborough

Captain James Cook was one of the greatest of all the famous sailors who have set out from the shores of England to discover new lands.

His combined achievements as explorer, navigator, cartographer (map maker), and superb seaman, have never been surpassed.

Cook was born of poor parents in 1728, in the village of Marton in Yorkshire where his father worked on a farm. The boy had a simple education at a little school locally, but soon left to help his father. At the age of seventeen he left the farm and obtained work at a shop in the pretty fishing village and seaport of Staithes.

The shop sold grocery and haberdashery. Nearly everyone in Staithes however was connected with the sea, and everywhere there was talk of ships and seafaring. No doubt there were many times when James was delivering goods down by the harbour that he gazed with growing interest at the vessels coming and going, and listened to the fascinating tales of the sailors.

It was not long before he decided that a lifetime behind a counter was not for him. In 1746, at the age of eighteen, he left the shop for a life at sea.

It was a momentous decision that led to great and important results. Before James Cook died he was to see more of the world than any man had seen before.

The young James Cook grows interested in ships and a life at sea

With the help of Mr Saunderson, the shop owner – an understanding man – James Cook was apprenticed to John and Henry Walker, coal shippers of Whitby. The ships owned by the Walkers were called colliers, and were specially built for carrying coal between ports up and down the east coast.

They were clumsy and wide, but could carry large quantities of cargo in the big holds. In spite of being slow and poor sailers, except when the wind was very favourable, they had good sea-keeping qualities and were able to ride out the fiercest gale.

So perhaps it is not surprising to find that one of these vessels was later chosen to take Cook and the scientists of the Royal Society on the first great voyage of discovery to the South Seas.

Cook's first ship was called the *Freelove*. Life in any collier must have been hard and rough, yet it was whilst sailing in her that he began to study navigation. This is the science of finding your way at sea by observation of the sun and stars. To do this it is necessary to have a knowledge of mathematics, including geometry. No easy task for a young man with little schooling! Yet it is recorded that Cook spent every spare moment, particularly when ashore, studying to improve his knowledge.

James Cook sets foot on his first ship, the Freelove

The Walkers admired the young man and they became firm friends. When the opportunity arose he was made one of the officers of their new ship, the *Friendship*, and for the next three years he sailed as mate, trading across the North Sea to the ports of Norway and the Baltic.

This was very good training for the man who was later to sail all around the world, because the North Sea is often covered by thick fog, and a sailor has to be a good navigator to keep on course.

Cook was a very good officer and certainly knew more about navigation than anyone else employed by the Walker brothers in their ships. When the captain of the *Friendship* left, Cook was offered the ship in his place. This was a fine chance for a young man of twenty seven, and shows how much the owners were impressed by his abilities as a seaman and navigator. But to everyone's astonishment, Cook refused the offer and, instead, joined the Royal Navy.

It seemed an incredible choice. Life in an eighteenth century man-of-war was both primitive and brutal, amongst men who had been press-ganged into service. Cook himself has left no record of his reasons, but perhaps he saw no future in the collier trade, and realised that in the Navy there would be greater opportunities to further his ambitions.

*Navigating in thick fog on the North Sea
gave Cook his first practical experience*

In 1755 the long expected war began between England and France over possession of the great new lands overseas, Canada and India. Cook's ship, the 60 gun *Eagle*, was sent to blockade the French ports to prevent French ships from leaving with supplies and reinforcements for their troops overseas.

Although Cook had turned down the opportunity of being captain of a vessel for the lowly rank of able seaman in a naval ship, he did not remain long in that position.

During wartime, as the number of naval ships increased, officers and men were urgently needed. Cook's outstanding abilities were certainly noticed very quickly for within a month he was appointed to

the position of master's mate.

Cook was aboard the *Eagle* when a fierce fight occurred with a large French 50 gun merchantman, named the *Duc d'Aquitaine*. After a running battle the French ship was crippled and captured. This was the only major sea fight that Cook was ever engaged in. The important part is that, throughout this period at sea, he was gradually improving the already exceptional skills of navigation and seamanship that he possessed.

In a remarkably short time of just over two years he rose from seaman to master's mate, to boatswain, and at last to master, the man in charge of the actual running of the ship.

With the rank of master, Cook was transferred to a larger ship, *HMS Pembroke*, which in February, 1758 joined the fleet sailing to attack the French in Canada.

The war had not gone well for the British in the American colonies, for a British army under General Braddock had been defeated and routed by the French and their Indian allies. The British government's plan was to attack the French in Canada and thus take the pressure off the colonies further south.

If you look at a map of North America you will see a great river, the St Lawrence, joining the five great lakes with the sea. This river runs between Canada

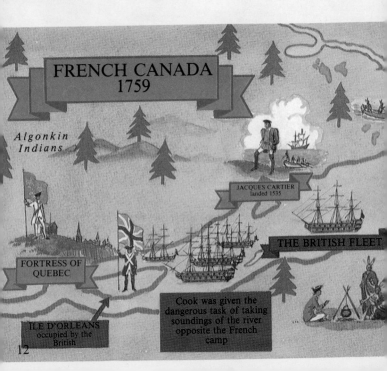

FRENCH CANADA
1759

Algonkin Indians

JACQUES CARTIER
landed 1535

THE BRITISH FLEET

FORTRESS OF QUEBEC

ILE D'ORLEANS
occupied by the British

Cook was given the dangerous task of taking soundings of the river opposite the French camp

and what is now the United States of America, but when Cook sailed in the *Pembroke*, it was held by the French. The fleet had orders to sail up the St Lawrence and attack the main French fortress at Quebec.

The St Lawrence is very wide and there are many islands and shallow places. Cook proved so good at finding the right channels that when the ships had sailed up to Quebec, he was sent for by General Wolfe, who commanded the British forces. The task the General gave to Cook was vital and important. It shows that Cook's skill as a navigator was already being recognised by the authorities.

First Christian Mission site

St Lawrence River

Following the success of the British in Canada, Cook was given the task of surveying the river from Quebec to the sea.

Malecite Indians

13

Quebec is situated on high ground overlooking the river. The only way the British could attack was from the river and to do this the soldiers had to be landed from the big ships in small boats.

The St Lawrence river at this point is extremely difficult to navigate. It is a maze of shoals and rocks and shifting sandbars, and highly dangerous to any ships unless the channels are accurately marked. Naturally the French had removed the buoys, and Cook's task was to discover where the safe channels lay.

This meant he had to go in a small boat, take soundings of the river to find out how deep the water was, then mark the shallow places on a chart. It was a difficult and dangerous task. Yet the charts he produced were so painstaking and accurate that over two hundred British ships were able to sail up the river and anchor near Quebec without mishap.

To add to the difficulties much of the work had to be done in the dark, as Cook was frequently in range of the French guns.

On one occasion he was nearly caught when a number of Indians in swift canoes put out from the French shore. Just in time he reached a British-held island and escaped.

Charting the St Lawrence River was a difficult and dangerous task, made more so by the threat of attack by Indians

General James Wolfe was a brilliant and determined commander beloved by his men. It is certain that he recognised in Cook a man of similar brilliant qualities.

The task of taking the great fortified citadel, protected by high cliffs and the river, seemed impossible. Wolfe decided the only way was to climb the cliffs at night, assemble on the plain above and force the French general, Montcalm, to give battle.

The plan worked well. In the early part of the night, small boats ferried the troops to the tiny beach. Above them towered the cliffs known as the Heights of Abraham. In the darkness the soldiers began the perilous climb up the steep and slippery path. By dawn the small army was in position on top of the cliffs and the astonished French awoke to see the British force awaiting them.

With considerable haste Montcalm assembled his troops and marched out to do battle. The British waited until the French drew close, then fired volley after volley, throwing the French back in confusion. Wolfe saw that this was the moment to attack and led the way forward.

He was killed at the moment of victory, but before he died he knew the battle was won and that henceforth Canada would belong to the British. The success was partly due to Cook's great skill in charting the river so accurately.

Climbing the Heights of Abraham

Canada now became a British possession. Today it is a self-governing Dominion, part of the great British Commonweath of Nations.

Cook was promoted and employed in charting the St Lawrence river below Quebec. This work is known as marine surveying, and consists of making maps of the coast as well as the shape and depth of the bottom of the sea near the coast. It is very important that this should be done carefully and accurately. If it is not, sailors who are steering by the maps, or charts as they are called, can very easily be wrecked.

In many places the St Lawrence is miles wide. Making a chart meant long days out in a small boat, taking soundings of the depth of the water. Every sandbank and channel had to be in exactly the right position on the chart.

This was done by taking the compass bearing of two or more prominent land features – then drawing the directional lines on the chart. Where the lines met was Cook's position, and month after month was spent taking thousands of soundings. When completed the charts were so successful and accurate that they were published by the Admiralty.

The capture of Canada had brought to England vast new territories, including the large island of Newfoundland, and new charts of the coast were needed by the Admiralty.

Cook was ordered to prepare them and made 'Marine Surveyor of the coast of Newfoundland and Labrador,' a post he held for four years. He was also given command of a ship of his own, the schooner *Grenville*, his first command.

During this time he published books of sailing directions of remarkable quality, and attracted the attention of the Royal Society by an account of the eclipse of the sun.

An eclipse of the sun is caused by the moon passing exactly between the earth and the sun, so that it is just as though the sun was blotted out of the sky. It is an important event in astronomy and is always very carefully observed.

It is possible to tell beforehand when an eclipse will take place and Cook knew that he would be able to see it perfectly on August 5th, 1766 from a small island just to the south of Newfoundland.

That the account written by Cook should be accepted by the Royal Society as accurate shows that he was now highly proficient in practical astronomy in relation to navigation.

The stage was thus set for further advancement.

Cook observes an eclipse of the sun in 1766

Some members of the scientific party

Sydney Parkinson (artist)

Joseph Banks (botanist)

Dr Carl Solander (botanist)

Some three years after the observations in Canada, Cook was chosen for another expedition to observe a similar event.

This was a transit of Venus.

Venus is one of the planets which, like our earth, go round the sun. A transit of Venus is really exactly like an eclipse of the sun, except that it is Venus which passes between the earth and the sun, and not the moon. Because Venus is so much further away from us than the moon, it does not blot out the sun. It appears merely as a small black dot crossing its face.

The best place from which to observe this transit of Venus was on an island called Tahiti, in the South Pacific Ocean.

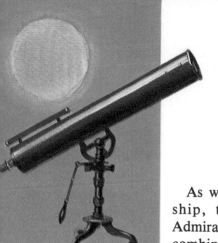

Special telescope used to observe Venus

As well as providing the ship, the Lords of the Admiralty also decided to combine the astronomical event with a great voyage of discovery in the unknown seas to the south. The natural choice to lead such an expedition was James Cook.

The scientists appointed by the Royal Society to accompany the ship included Joseph Banks – later to become Sir Joseph and the Society's president – and Charles Green, the official astronomer for the actual observation of the transit. Artists and botanists also accompanied the expedition.

Cook used a quadrant such as this when navigating. (It is used to measure the height of the sun or the stars above the horizon)

The ship chosen for the voyage was a converted Whitby collier named the *Endeavour,* a type of vessel that Cook knew well from his earlier years at sea. It was to become one of the most famous ships ever to sail from an English port. But it was ridiculously small for the large number of people on board, plus the immense amount of stores and equipment necessary for the long voyage.

As well as the ship's officers, there were some forty seamen, several midshipmen – young men learning to be officers – and twelve marines, together with clerks and servants.

Among the scientific party was Dr Daniel Carl Solander, a famous botanist, and two artists named Alexander Buchan and Sydney Parkinson.

There were no photographs in those days and the only way to show what places and things looked like was by drawing and painting them. This was the artists' responsibility. Buchan was a landscape painter and his task was to paint scenes of the various places they visited; Parkinson was employed mainly in drawing the natural history specimens found on the voyage.

And the scientists, Banks and Solander, deserved every praise for their work and for the hundreds of specimens of fish, birds, insects and plants, previously unknown in Europe, that were collected, preserved and brought back to England.

Sydney Parkinson made careful drawings of the bird, plant and animal life

The *Endeavour* reached Tahiti on April 13th, 1769, and as the ship entered the bay scores of canoes came out to meet it. The natives were friendly and happy and Cook and the scientists were delighted with the beauty and atmosphere of the island.

However, they soon found out that Tahitians were inclined to steal anything that took their fancy and this, unfortunately, led to trouble. Preparations to observe the transit of Venus from the shore got under way and a fort of palisades and earthworks was constructed on the north side of the bay. Sentries guarded the tents and scientific equipment inside. Nevertheless, it was found that the quadrant, a most important instrument essential for the observation, had disappeared. Cook had to take stern measures before it was recovered.

The transit was successfully observed, but the results had little scientific value. The astronomical instruments of that time were just not accurate enough.

Having carefully charted Tahiti and the nearby islands and named them the Society Islands (because they are so close together) Cook sailed for the south. About 1,500 miles were covered without sight of land. There was certainly no sign of the great southern continent that was supposed to exist, and at last the *Endeavour* turned and headed west — towards New Zealand.

At Tahiti, Cook was welcomed by friendly natives

New Zealand was first sighted about a century previously, by a Dutch navigator named Tasman. The island of Tasmania is named after him. But although Tasman sailed for some distance along the west coast, he did not sail far enough south to discover whether New Zealand was an island or part of a large southern continent. It was left to James Cook to establish that it was, in fact, two large islands divided by a strait (Cook's Strait: now Cook Strait).

Cook sailed completely round both islands, charting the coastline as he went, and naming the various bays and headlands – names which remain to this day. He and some of his men were the first Europeans

to set foot on New Zealand soil, for Tasman had found the natives so hostile he never attempted to land.

Unfortunately they were also hostile when Cook went ashore, and the first landing resulted in a skirmish. Cook tried again, with a similar result. When he had himself rowed round the bay to look for a place where they could land unopposed, they were attacked by warriors in canoes and had to open fire in self defence.

Cook was appalled by the fighting, for his policy was to make friends with the inhabitants of the islands and in most cases he was successful.

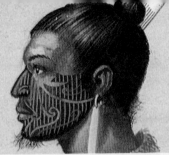

Maori warriors

The natives of New Zealand are called Maoris: a strongly-built race with light brown skins. At that time they were still a primitive people using stone tools with great skill, becoming particularly adept at wood carving.

The adze, in various sizes, was the principal tool for this work. It is an axe-like tool, but whereas the axe has the blade set in line with the handle, the blade of the adze is set across, and it is used to chip away at the surface of the wood. The blade of the Maori adze was of very hard stone.

They practised agriculture and lived in village settlements, some of which were fortified with a palisade, but not all Maoris were hostile to the

Maori carving

newcomers. When Cook landed in other areas, many of the natives were friendly and willing to trade.

After the long voyage and the gale force winds and rough weather experienced since leaving Tahiti, the *Endeavour* was beginning to leak badly. Cook had to find a place where the ship could be careened.

This meant hauling the ship up on to a suitable sandy beach, scraping all the barnacles and other marine growth from the bottom, and then recaulking the joints between the planking to make it watertight again.

Maori chieftain

The expedition had now accomplished everything it had been asked to do, and with the ship seaworthy again all was ready for the return voyage to England.

It was typical of Cook that he decided to sail home by way of another largely unexplored area — the east coast of Australia.

Lieutenant Hicks was first to sight Australia

The existence of the great continent was already known. It had been named 'New Holland' by the early Dutch navigators, who were probably the first Europeans to actually land there. Tasman had sailed along parts of the north and west coasts, but beyond that little else was known of its size or extent.

The *Endeavour* left New Zealand on April 1st, 1770 and headed west for Van Diemen's Land, the island we now call Tasmania. At the time this was thought to be part of the Australian mainland. When Tasman had charted its position over a century before, he had not sailed sufficiently far round the coast to realise that it was not attached to Australia.

Cook also missed this fact, for southerly gales forced his ship to the north away from Tasmania. At six o'clock on the morning of April 19th, land was sighted about fifteen miles distant, and was named Point Hicks after Lieutenant Hicks who saw it first. It was the south-eastern tip of Australia.

Cook now sailed north along the coast for several days looking for a suitable harbour.

At times smoke was seen, which showed the region was inhabited, but it was not until a week had passed that they saw some figures on the shore. Cook with several companions set off in the yawl, but when they were still some distance away the natives ran off into the woods. The boat was unable to land because of the heavy surf.

Returning to the ship they set sail again, eventually coming to a fine large bay where they anchored.

Here they met their first Australian aborigines. A few were hostile and threw spears at the boats while others — to Cook's astonishment — seemed completely indifferent. The crew left a few presents of beads, pieces of cloth and ribbons but the natives kept their distance.

The white men noticed that all the native men carried a kind of 'short scimitar' — which proved to be the famous boomerang.

For the scientists, Joseph Banks, Dr Solander and the others it was a marvellous place. The bay teemed with fish, and hundreds of plants and shrubs were found that were quite unknown in Europe. So much so that Cook gave it the name — which later became notorious as the convict settlement — Botany Bay.

Captain Cook and his party of scientists land at Botany Bay

Leaving Botany Bay the *Endeavour* sailed north for five weeks, with Cook busy surveying and charting the coastline as they passed.

But this coast was unlike any that he had ever seen before. A great reef of coral, called the Great Barrier Reef, stretches up the north-east coast of Australia for hundreds of miles. Cook sailed between it and the shore, but he was of course without any charts to guide him. One night, without any warning, the ship struck on the reef and remained fast.

The situation was desperate. They were on an unknown coast thousands of miles from home. Stores, ballast and even some guns were thrown overboard to lighten the vessel. When at last, after immense effort, the ship floated clear it was feared it would sink as water was coming in fast. Luckily a large chunk of coral had broken off and partly plugged the hole. With a struggle they managed to reach the mainland where the ship was beached and the damaged hull repaired.

The voyage was resumed but before leaving the northernmost cape of Australia, Cook landed and hoisted the British flag.

By doing this he claimed Australia for Britain, and it remains today, like Canada, a great self-governing Dominion in the British Commonwealth.

Aground on the Great Barrier Reef

The *Endeavour* arrived in England having been away from home for two years and eleven months. During this time Cook had done more to increase man's knowledge of the Pacific and the southern seas than any man had ever done before.

But his achievements did not end there. In an age when half the crew of a ship would expect to die from scurvy on a long voyage, Cook had not lost a single man from that dreaded disease.

Scurvy is a sickness which attacks people when they live on a monotonous diet without vegetables or fruit. On the old sailing ships the food consisted almost entirely of meat salted down in barrels, and of hard ship's biscuit. Of course, fresh vegetables could not be obtained when the ship was away from land for months.

Cook's method of preventing scurvy was to take a supply of 'sauerkraut', a sort of pickled vegetable, on his voyages. This provided the necessary vitamins.

At first the sailors would not eat it, so Cook gave orders that it was only to be served to the officers. After that all the crew wanted it!

He also insisted on a hygienic routine for the ship — something unheard-of in those days. Fresh air and cleanliness in the cramped quarters between decks, dry clothes when possible, personal cleanliness and, again when possible, a supply of lemons which were known to help in preventing scurvy.

The crew want their sauerkraut!

Cook was not in England for very long. A year later he was again at sea, once more searching for the great southern continent.

Two ships were provided for this expedition — the *Resolution* commanded by Cook, and the *Adventure*, commanded by Tobias Furneaux. They eventually became separated in a thick fog and Cook continued the voyage alone.

It had long been thought that a few hundred miles south of New Zealand and South Africa lay another great mass of land — another continent. No one had seen it but it was pictured on old maps as a vague cloudy shape.

On this second tremendous voyage of exploration, Cook sailed completely round the world, going further south than anyone had been before. He proved once and for all that the great southern continent did not exist.

In that part of the world it was all ocean. A vast, empty expanse of sea, subject to great winds and storms.

Unhindered by land, gigantic waves built up, tossing the small vessel about like a cork. It was a time of great hardship for everyone on board. Everything was soaking wet the whole time and it was almost impossible to have any hot food with the constant pitching and rolling of the ship.

After weeks of sailing in the icy waters of the South Polar seas, Cook was forced by bad weather and the extreme cold of the Antarctic to turn north and make for New Zealand.

Here he was reunited with the *Adventure* whose crew was suffering from scurvy. Cook cured this, and the two ships went on to explore several Pacific islands, only to be separated once more in a howling gale as they returned to New Zealand. After waiting over three weeks Cook left New Zealand on 8th October to continue the journey alone. (The *Adventure* had in fact suffered some misfortune and returned to England.) There followed several months of sailing, sometimes far south among the icebergs, before turning north again.

On March 12th, 1774 the ship reached one of the strangest islands in the world. It is known as Easter Island. This lonely spot lies far south in the Pacific Ocean and it contains a mystery that is still unsolved. For scattered all over this small barren island are scores of huge stone statues.

No one knows why or when they were made, or who made them. But it is certain that the men who carved them out of the soft rock had no metal tools. Nor had they any means of moving them other than hauling them with ropes made of grass.

Some of these statues are thirty feet high and weigh fifty tons. They still remain today where they have stood for hundreds of years, looking out over the sea.

The mysterious statues on Easter Island

Cook had now covered almost three-quarters of the globe in his exploration of the southern oceans and had sailed nearer to the South Pole than anyone had been before.

In addition he had made tremendous sweeps into the Pacific that had taken him from the icy waters of the Polar Seas almost to the Equator. And all this in a small, clumsy, slow-moving sailing ship!

At last, after a final visit to New Zealand, the *Resolution* headed east.

Five weeks and 4,500 miles later, the tip of South America was reached, Cape Horn was passed and the ship sailed on into the South Atlantic. Three more weeks passed and Cook reached the point where he had first entered the Antarctic Circle two years before. He had circumnavigated the world further

south than anyone had thought possible.

Upon his return to England Cook was acknowledged as the greatest navigator of the age, and was suitably honoured.

He was made a Fellow of the Royal Society, received by King Georgé III, presented with a gold medal for his paper on health at sea, and appointed to the well-paid post of Captain at Greenwich Hospital (this was a home for naval pensioners rather than a hospital).

He was now forty seven years old and could have lived in comfortable retirement for the rest of his life at Greenwich.

But plans for yet another great voyage were already being considered by the Admiralty.

he Resolution *in the Antarctic*

This third voyage was to search for a possible sea-route between the Atlantic and Pacific Oceans round the north of Canada. For two centuries mariners had tried to find this North-West Passage, as it was called, but all previous attempts had failed.

Now it was planned that Cook should search for a way from the Pacific side, while another attempt was to be made from the Atlantic at the same time.

Cook left Plymouth with two ships, the *Resolution* and the *Discovery*. He sailed via South Africa and New Zealand, then across the Pacific, reaching the west coast of North America in March, 1778.

Gradually they felt their way northward, finally passing through the Bering Straits and on into the Arctic Circle, where further progress was halted by unbroken ice that stretched to the horizon. There was no way of getting through.

With the cold increasing and the danger of being iced in for months, Cook returned to the Bering Straits and crossed over to Asia. There he met some friendly Russian sailors and fur hunters. Neither spoke the other's language but the Russians could understand charts and were able to give Cook some useful information.

With further exploration impossible in the north, Cook decided to go south to the Sandwich Islands for the winter and renew the search for a North-West Passage the following spring.

The Russian sailors help Cook

The Sandwich Islands, now known as the Hawaiian Islands, had been discovered by Cook earlier in the year on his way to the north.

It was his last important discovery. The ships had stopped at one of the islands for water and fresh provisions, and had found the natives friendly and attractive.

On the return visit the island of Maui, second largest in the group, was sighted first and after a pause, the ships sailed on to the main island, Hawaii. The news of their coming had preceded them.

Here they received a royal welcome and Cook was persuaded to take part in an elaborate ceremony, which, although he did not fully realise it, made him a god in the eyes of the people.

According to Hawaiian legend one of their gods, Lono, the god of happiness, peace and agriculture, had sailed away across the sea ages ago but one day was expected to return. The natives thought Cook was Lono come home again.

Wherever he went he was treated like a god with ceremonies and offerings. Large quantities of bread fruit, yams, sugar cane and hogs were continually presented to the ships.

After the most friendly of visits, Cook sailed once more, intending to complete a survey of the islands before making a second attempt to find a North-West Passage during the summer months.

The natives believed Cook was a god, and worshipped him

The ships did not get far. A severe gale damaged the foremast of the *Resolution* and forced them to return to Hawaii for repairs. There was no reason to think the islanders would not welcome them again, but it was clear that their attitude had changed.

The friendliness was no longer in evidence. It is possible that seeing the damaged ship limping back they realised that Cook was no god. Or possibly the priests were jealous and did not want to take second place again.

Several acts of thieving caused further trouble, and a scuffle developed when the sailors tried to get the property back. That night one of the ship's boats was

Cook is killed by a native in Hawaii

stolen. Next morning, 14th February 1779, Cook went ashore with armed marines with the intention of holding the chief hostage until the boat and other items were recovered. A huge crowd gathered on the beach and during a moment when Cook was separated from his men, shots were heard from further along the shore. An armed warrior came at Cook, and Cook fired. The marines opened fire and soon the fighting was hand to hand. As Cook turned to signal to the boats he was struck down and killed.

In this tragic way Captain James Cook died. Endowed with a keen intelligence, great character, energy and outstanding ability, he was the finest navigator the world has known.

INDEX